Minsk

LAVINIA GREENLAW

Minsk

POEMS

HARCOURT, INC.

Orlando ★ Austin ★ New York ★ San Diego ★ Toronto ★ London

Requests for permission to make copies of any part of the work
should be mailed to the following address:
Permissions Department, Harcourt, Inc.,
6277 Sea Harbor Drive, Orlando, Florida 32887-6777.

www.HarcourtBooks.com

First published in Great Britain by Faber & Faber in 2003.

Library of Congress Cataloging-in-Publication Data
Greenlaw, Lavinia, 1962–
Minsk: poems/Lavinia Greenlaw.
p.   cm.
I. Title.
PR6057.R375M56 2005
821'.914—dc22   2004029402
ISBN-10: 0-15-101092-7
ISBN-13: 978-0-15-101092-9

Text set in Dante
Designed by Scott Piehl

Printed in the United States of America

First U.S. edition
A C E G I K J H F D B

for my mother and father,
my brothers and sister

CONTENTS

THE LAND OF GIVING IN

FOREWORD

Edward Hirsch

Lavinia Greenlaw is a precisionist. Her work is exact and exacting, thoughtful and thought-provoking, filled with invention and ideas. She has a deceptively light touch, a natural reticence, and a characteristically oblique manner. She is all tact and gravity. Her style is so taut and elliptical, so deft, laconic, and shapely, so clever and pleasurable, that it takes a while to see that her vision is also uncompromising. She resists fixing things in ice, but she can also be chillingly truthful.

Greenlaw writes with what Vladimir Nabokov called "a merging of the precision of poetry and the intuition of science." Her formal control is formidable. She admires symmetries and supplies them. She is keenly observant, descriptively acute, self-consciously concise. Her writing has a classical austerity and balance. She is fascinated by issues of time and space. Landscapes matter to her, and so do the actual mechanics of perception. She has evidently learned a great deal from Elizabeth Bishop, her first model. Indeed, what she has said of Bishop seems true of herself as well. "Her observations are so patient and particular, but full of excitement, engagement, the active nature of looking...She is clear, disturbed and determined: 'all the untidy activity continues,/awful but cheerful.'" Greenlaw's work, like Bishop's, often feels restrained and cool to the touch, though it, too, has a secret electricity—dark undertows, radioactive depths. It is morally charged.

Greenlaw's first book, *Night Photograph* (1993), is notable for its unusually adept use of subjects and metaphors drawn from science. The poems themselves maintain a steady pace, the rhythm of quiet discovery. One feels that they are a bit like the trio of missiles that the poet discovers on the road to Jericho:

> This was a precise migration—
> linear, parallel, constant.
> An exact miracle
> on a straight road
> over flat land
> under clear sky.

Greenlaw's sparse poems have grown more complicated and adventurous over the years, but she retains a sense of calibration and measurement, a feeling for mathematical beauty, an appreciation for the precise shape of things. Her second book, *A World Where News Travelled Slowly* (1997), is more personal and wayward, more restless and immoderate. ("Moderation in moderation. Who said that?/It makes extraordinary sense to me.") She continues to try to find, as an early poem formulated it, "some wild enlightenment" that can only be achieved with an "eye for detail" ("Science for Poets"). Yet she has also pushed herself into deeper and more unpredictable waters. She has become looser and poetically freer, more emotionally open, something more of a seeker, a dreamer facing north—hence the title of her third and best book thus far, her breakthrough volume, *Minsk*.

Greenlaw is a winter writer and her landscapes are icy

ones, bleak places where she can determine and explore questions of place. Her work has a cold beauty. She remembers landscapes of childhood, especially London and Essex, travels to the far north, the realm of the Arctic Circle ("Arctic winter has set in my body/like a drink of glass") and daydreams about faraway Belarus. As she formulates it in "Sisu":

> To love winter.
> To adapt to its broken promise.
> To persevere in hope of summer.

The speaker in her poems is terrified of stasis, striking out across "ploughed and frozen earth" ("Zombies"), trying to break through the frosty pane of glass that always seems to separate her from the world. Hence her fond and even loving memory of being suspended in air:

THE FALLING CITY

> I was eight, I was atmosphere,
> more than willing to take to the air.
> The world was locked and clear.
>
> For a moment the glass forgave me,
> curved like a hand that absolutely
> loved me, let me down so gently.

It is "not love of winter," she writes in her poem "Camel Hair," "but a loss of the feel of the world,/a way ahead of the cold."

What I especially love about this book is its hard-won clarity and wisdom, its Stevensian dream of what is absent from our lives, the lost land, the fantasy of the farthest point north, the Minsk of our imaginations, which includes "A home upon a golden hill/with city gates of straw and strawheaded children." This book is a journey, and the reader, like the writer, comes away from the frozen tundra with a deeper sense of our emotional need for warmth. We map and record, which, like the Arctic sunset, "looks easy, but hurts." We turn back southward. "My heart bursts with joy, every cell," Greenlaw writes in "Heliotropical," "and the light comes still." In the end, the brightness of this book burns. The afterglow remains.

I

Your homecoming will be my homecoming.

—E. E. CUMMINGS

THE SPIRIT OF THE STAIRCASE

In our game of flight, half-way down
was as near mid-air as it got: a point
of no return we'd fling ourselves at
over and over, riding pillows or trays.
We were quick to smooth the edge
of every step, grinding the carpet to glass
on which we'd lose our grip.
The new stairs were our new toy,
the descent to an odd extension,
four new rooms at flood level
in a sunken garden—a wing
dislocated from a hive. Young bees
with soft stripes and borderless nights,
we'd so far been squared away
in a twin-set of bunkbeds, so tight-knit,
my brother and I once woke up finishing
a conversation begun in a dream.
It had been the simplest exchange,
one I'd give much to return to:
the greetings of shadows unsurprised
at having met beneath the trees
and happy to set off again, alone,
back into the dark.

THE FALLING CITY

I was eight, I was atmosphere,
more than willing to take to the air.
The world was locked and clear.

For a moment the glass forgave me,
curved like a hand that absolutely
loved me, let me down so gently.

THE DISSECTION ROOM

My mother's eyes were behind glass,
preternaturally unblinking, flexed.
In the fifties, hieroglyphic contact lenses

—watertight, they swivelled like a pair
of monumental but well-oiled radar
homing in on the senior student (my father),

whose sight was fixed on the blue blood
struggling to circulate in her hand
as she rolled on a glove to dip a finger

in a dead man's chest, then threw a blinder
with her photographic recall: a text-book case
of *dextrocardia,* heart in the wrong place.

Who could tell if what she was groping for
was a misericord or, failing that, a rip cord?

THE PARACHUTE

There is a place in Hell that's known as the Malebolge, all
of iron-grey stone walled in by its own iron-grey stone.

    —*Inferno,* CANTO XVIII, 1–3

Too many things fell out of the sky.
A family curse—satanic, genetic.

So what to make of the gift
of an army-issue collapsible moped

dropped behind enemy lines?
Requisitioned debutante

turned rebel medical student,
she applied a membrane of nail-polish pink

enamel, which faltered
as she revved up to circle Parliament Square,

the *mala bolgia*
beneath her father's grace-and-favour window.

If only that veneer
had billowed and resisted the air

like the caul of her second son, so intact
that her doctor husband shook

as he tore him open,
the last of his unfinishable children

who made a study of each other's nerves,
all four born witch-hunters.

LUPINS

'That girl's uncomfortable just being inside
her own skin.' Wolves comforted me.
I grew up within earshot.

Their howls would climb the hill
like tall spikes of blue flowers,
as if the zoo's iron railings

had unfurled beneath their spell.
Traffic gets up across the canal.
Some slip through lights

like baby golden tamarin monkeys.
Others wait, baffled clownfish
behind glass.

THE LONG DAY CLOSES

Pulled from my shell of dreams and noise,
I was taken to live in a quiet place
where the undiluted dark of the streets
without streetlight, had no emphasis.

Boys on boys' shoulders turned
the crossroads signpost back, conferred
on baffled drivers four blind corners,
an added hour of English winter.

Power cuts shut the short days down.
I moved my bed against the boards
that hid the chimney, kindled warmth
and probed the heater's one grey bar.

(I near enough went up in smoke,
the shock made metal of my bones,
suspended me in its dead boom.)
We were ancients, reading flames,

trimming wicks and filling wells with oil.
I hacked crow feathers into quills,
cooked up a raw and bloody ink,
a berry tincture so red-gold,

my scratched-out maps of cities glowed
like city night, then dried intro scrolls
I sealed with wax that once ignited,
hissed and spat like a fuse...

The girls at school ironed their hair
while mine writhed in snakes. I stared
myself to stone. My vision failed:
things went first at the edges, fields

flooded fields, chalk lifted off from boards
like snow from mountains, came apart
through distance, like the wiped faces
my eyes could not now reach.

BLACKWATER

Where the coastline doubles up on itself
as if punched in the gut by the god Meander,
who likes to dabble in landscapes
but, with this one, lost his grip.
He muddled salt and sweet,
bent the creeks more than double,
loaded each distinction
till it burst its banks. Picture this:
an estuary where the eye can't tell
sea from river, hill from valley,
near from far, first from last, in from out
—any one thing, in fact, from any other.

Where the stumps of Saxon fishtraps
butt up through the silt at low tide
like the rusted teeth in the wrecked head
of the god Yawn, who can't keep his mouth shut,
not here, where the land spits out
its haul of the useless,
the shapeless,
tasteless, nameless.

Where there has been nothing as clear
as the winter in which the goddess Inertia
hunkered down over Maldon
—the town hemmed in with skirts of ice.
The men of the saltworks and oyster pits,
bass fishers, whelk pickers, farmers and bargees

were hamstrung. Some set off
to find the first three miles in any direction
glass, their boats sleeved in glass,
glass hobbling their horses.

Where the vague men of the Dengie Peninsula
drove their marsh lambs a fortnight's walk
to market and picked up a wife on the way:
an inland girl from a county town
whose clean lungs became damp rooms,
whose good skin leathered and would not cure,
whose blood was drunk by the god Stagnant
who came at night and took little sips
till her blackened soul left her body,
how else, but by way of water.

Where you think you've reached open sea
till something catches in your throat
—fossil fuel and fish long out of water,
where the goddess Stasis laid a path
towards the horizon, which seems not far
till you sidle, circle, give up, settle in
like the World War One submarines
docked in the shallows near Osea.
Unactivated, they grew so at home
that Stasis offered them the gift of life
as mud lumps on mud banks
who honk and puff their way off shore.
Reborn, they zoom to the battle zone
(where Osea keeps watch on Ostend)

drawn to the mutating warmth
of Bradwell power station's radiant pools.

Where they at last unplugged the glottal stop
in the throat of the god Moribund
and opened a wall to unravel the fields
where the borrow dyke lends itself to the polder,
mops up sticklebacks and sea lavender:
—bristling, stunted, salt and sweet.

Where the county arms are three cutlasses,
each with a bite taken out
by a bored god. Salt of earth,
they chew the matter over:
'Whatever's it all about, John?'
'Whenever is it all going to end?'

ESSEX RAG

Do not play this piece fast.
It is never right to play ragtime fast.

—SCOTT JOPLIN

The piano years... Too young to drive
I played pedal to the metal,
full reverb, wah-wah and fuzz,
a collision course bending *Chopsticks*
into hairpins, trilling the hell
out of cheesy *Für Elise.*

The teacher's 'grown-up' bait
was a bowdlerised *Ode to Joy,*
heavy goods I slammed through,
dropping a trail of exhausted parts
—like the juggernauts
shouldering the lane past our door.

If the point is not to bring the house down,
what better place
than somewhere you wake up
to everything years after it's moved on?
The times I tried to move on...
But from here, I mean there, wherever

you get to is not far and still nowhere, so
there's nothing for it but to head home,

unsure whether the last bus has gone.
There's slow and there's the discovery of slow.
The last bus has not gone.
It never comes.

CLOWNFISH

So bored we made a film of our lives
and played ourselves—botched reincarnations
of doctors, madmen, evangelists and spies.
The set was the holding tank, a room so void
that it gargled the dross bubbling up
from waist-high, silted, oracular speakers.
Adolescents drowning in our own soup,
we crooned their baggy truths...
Only we knew how to dance The Hoe,
how to unrhyme slang, the rules, the angle,
the camber in the mini-snooker's baize,
the warp and dimples of the ping-pong table,
the laws of croquet on a scuffed, erupting lawn.
We lived smack dab in the village eye,
bubbling up to mouth obscene charms
from the ousted admiral's port hole;
we ran nothing up his flag pole.
Low Celts with Viking horizons,
we torched the privet ship he'd clipped into shape
in a week. Our invasion was meant to repel.
My mother opened a fête, then lit a fuse:
Taxes for Peace, telegrams for Amnesty,
lifts for strangers, the communist vote.
She left *Protest and Survive* by the phone.
Neither ever occurred to us,
trailing one another's reputations
through the same barely resuscitated school
to return uprooted, re-accented but armed

with four bent pokers, four woodworks
in identical abstract free-form, to wait
for an end I imagined like the death of Hercules,
my mouldering goldfish, who stuck it out
so long that when he went belly up,
some god draped a tea-towel over his bowl.

FOXTROT

Nothing like the hang-dog
I caught out in the green belt at dawn,
nosing his way along the hard shoulder,
a backwater teenager hitching home,

fair game
for the double-act coming off night patrol,
open-armed, under-performed
and aching to croon into their cold radio:

'Foxtrot Alpha Sierra Tango'.
A chance to turn the lights down low,
to sharpen fancy moves that don't show,
taking it slow, slow, slow-slow, slow...

ZOMBIES

1980, I was returned to the city exposed
in black and white as the lights went on and on.
A back-alley neon sign, the first I'd seen,
drew us sweetly down and in to brightness:
a doll's parasol, a spike of green cherries,
the physic of apricot brandy, actual limes
and morning-to-night shades of rum.
Newly old enough and government-moneyed,
we knocked them back, melting the ice
between us and the unaccustomed looseness
of being legitimate and free. What possessed us?
Was it the kick of spirits or the invisible syrup
in which they swam that worked in our veins,
charming us into a car and forty miles east

to the fields of our years of boredom...
Did we not remember the curse of this place?
How Sundays drank our blood as we watched
dry paint or the dust on the television screen.
How people died bursting out of a quiet life,
or from being written into a small world's stories.
Who can see such things and live to tell?
How we hunted all night for noise and love,
striking out once across ploughed and frozen earth,
lurching from rut to rut until at the edge
we smashed our way out through a hedge, to fall
eight feet to the road. Of course, we felt nothing.
Was it not ourselves who frightened us most?
As if brightness or sweetness could save us.

BATTERSEA DOJO

He lived on lupins steeped in water.

—PLINY THE ELDER ON PROTOGENES

The hardcore years.
Towers emptied on the strength of a rumour.
For all that, the skyline boomed like a graph.
Inside the walls, money grew on trees.

Barefoot, shaven, crop-headed, a neophyte,
most weeks I had my collar felt.
'Sorry, I thought you were...'
A twenty-year-old blur
hauled backwards out of the Ladies.
(Who was it rushed up in the dark to kiss
me, his long-lost boy?)

A hard man with a face in bloom,
sensei liked to play old-fashioned
with his signet ring, conspiracies and heft.
He asked me to pardon his French
as we sat depleted, topping up
on pints of water with a lager chaser.

I learnt to fold myself behind the punch,
retract first then force the twist,
two knuckles raised on a tucked thumb;
to see both ways, to prolong the arc
of a kick in the *kata*'s quick-quick slow.

My dappled forearms noted the force
of my knifehand and rising blocks.
In attack, I was taught to miss by inches.

I was wire.
I drank the blue air.
Towers emptied on the strength of a rumour.

A STRANGE BARN

Bunk
The Raven's Cage, 1827

A field tent or marquee, wire mesh
open to all weathers, catching the worst
of a mortar blast in the last war.

Cramped shadows.
Birds as pivoted as compass needles,
collecting damp

like the new serge uniforms
of Peel's boys in blue,
who, in this combustible world,

cannot keep up with
let alone enforce
the law of Stephenson's Rocket.

Spin

The Giraffe House, 1836

A cool exaggeration, five-metre doors
made reasonable with Roman arches.
An arrangement of parts, the giraffe
carries himself off, all height, no weight.

His ancestor arrived in London at the dawn
of transcendentalism and acetylene.
Walking from the dock to Regent's Park,
he freaked at the sight of a cow in Commercial Road.

Fellow ungulates, they met in the year
of the Arc de Triomphe, *The Pickwick Papers*
and the birth of the state of Arkansas,
feats of design.

Hush

The Mappin Terraces, 1913

The timber frame of a helter-skelter
smoothed over like the scandal
of the imperial wireless contract
the ministers insisted Marconi won.

A concrete cover-up
to make a mole hill of a mountain.
Gandhi arrested. The King's horse
lost on Emily Davidson.

Each bear prowled its slice of hill
as if it were inside a wheel; to stay still
would be to backslide or sidestep.
Everyone was doing the foxtrot.

Dancers, anglers, children's friends,
fractious, wary, teeth and claws
extracted. The Lords tried twice
to stop the Irish Home Rule Bill.

The last horsedrawn omnibus in Paris
failed to make it through the winter.
There were no bears in the Armory Show,
no bears in *Sons and Lovers* or *Le Grand Meaulnes.*

Hiss

The Reptile House, 1926

The birth of the box. Sub-specific
amphibians bask in the ether,
break up against backdrop.

Camouflage. At last
we've cracked it, gone sub-atomic,
where everything we can't see is happening.

And so we set off
into the disturbed air,
descending into a world of repeats.

Scat

The Penguin Pool, 1934

The penguins don't get it, this shallow blue eye,
cut-outs, swerves and jazzy lines;

two ramps linked in a lover's toast
while protocol ties the continent in knots.

They huddle on a slope and eat.
Scrubbed tiles and old whitewash reek.

'Keep out of the water, stick together,
store fat. Wait for new feathers.'

Flit
The Aviary, 1962

The air hums with promise,
missiles for Cuba, a contract for Concorde,
The Birds and *Blowin' In The Wind*...

An ibis nestles against a stanchion,
sprats turn on a ledge,
starlings gang up on a splattered willow

while peacocks forage like metal detectors,
giving small electrified shrieks,
alert to something unearthly.

Stomp

The Elephant Pavilion, 1965

The idea is a herd in a scrum
trumpeting out of fear or just for fun.
The Americans bombed North Vietnam.

Flower Power, mini skirts. Copper trunks
fizz out of the roof—oxidised air vents.
This is the age of stalled effervescence.

Hessian, spotlights. The interior
is à la mode—soft focus, circular.
Just a skull and howdah as a reminder.

II

Denn wir, wo wir fühlen, verflüchtigen; ach wir
atmen uns aus und dahin.

For we, when we feel, evaporate; oh, we
breathe ourselves out and away.

—RAINER MARIA RILKE

FAITH

Watching you walk off among the rock pools,
your gaze, a rapid adjustment of angles
as jittery and acute as a blackbird's,
I see how your black linen suit
makes you a preacher, or a preacher's son:

Edmund Gosse, wanting nothing so much
as to abandon his creationist father,
unable, perhaps, not to see further
than the cockles and anemones, the trilobites
you fear you believe were put there by God.

MEPHISTO

After a night in the cellar
Goethe returned to with Faust,
I am up in the air again,
cumulo-cirrus, thin ice, a voice
that is crushing and reasonable:
'Your little life...'

We fly over a river,
part frozen, part cracking up
at the end of a beautiful winter:
a three-month blinding heaven
that will leave its smallprint
and otherwise nothing on earth.

LACHESIS

Trigonocephalus lachesis. *The Surukuku snake...*
According to Hering, Lachesis is particularly suitable to
those of melancholic disposition... thinks she is some
one else, in the hands of a stronger power.

—JOHN HENRY CLARKE, *Materia Medica*

Upon conversion, the order
was not so much given as made.
A divided state.

Work ate its own celebration.
Nights kept secret.
I never heard the children.

Years later
I turned up that picture,
my face so grey, I took it for dust;

warming itself at my neck,
a coral snake, a remedy
he would not have in the house.

See how I fingered the key
of its colours—blood, bile and choler,
so as to know it from its brother

and whether my throat might flush
with the milk of kindness
or a dose of likeness.

A DAMSEL IN DISTRESS
after Wodehouse

whom she met without
she thoroughly disapproved
He, at least, she always felt

had exhibited at times
she had always felt sure
to injure the family

is the only man that offers
beast desire

assuming—that is

by no other spot except
to nobody, by nobody

Here your lover may wander
at the end

righteous indignation
he held the opinion that
who in his time had
as scarcely human

might be judicious to continue
so became him as this assault
of youth, had come to lock
you've never got

a common rowdy in the streets
'If you knew the circumsta'
are in print'

name in the papers
'The circumstances? They

CAMEL HAIR

Every few years it becomes
a question of backbone.

Anhedonia,
not love of winter

but a loss of the feel of the world,
a way ahead of the cold.

Even the cells refuse
to talk to one another.

As black and white
as a two-hour wait on the kerb

of a six-lane arterial road,
in a secondhand straw-coloured Dior coat,

for the last bus and its overload
to accelerate past out of its own

well-oiled backsplash.

THE SUN SESSIONS
after Otis Blackwell

'56.
Amphibious,
barely out of his tail.

Heart in his mouth. Don't.
Perhaps he is trying
to swallow it.

The bull-frogs on backing
inflate. Be true. Oo oo oo.
On the tough acoustic

of an empty pool. Don't.
To a heart. Doo wah.
That's cruel. Sha la la la.

De dum. I mean
cruel. Wo wo wo wo.
And true.

THE PARTIAL TRUTH

My father died the day that I was born.
I learned how not to look, what not to learn.

I leave the world so fast, I never see
the hand that locks up after hide the key.

I did not fall when I fell down the stairs.
Because I never have been safe, I'm scared.

LORD YARBOROUGH'S DEFENCE

The land
in question,
by the slow, gradual
and imperceptible projection,
alluvion, subsidence, and accretion
of ooze, soil, sand, and other matter, being
slowly, gradually, and by imperceptible increase,
in a long time cast up, deposited, and settled by and from
the flux and reflux of the tide and water of the sea in upon and against
the outside and extremity of the demesne lands of the manor, hath been formed,
and hath settled grown and accrued upon against and unto the said demesne lands.

THE FLIGHT OF GERYON
Inferno, *Canto xvii, 76–106*

What holds you back from the edge but fading spirits?
There's a way down, only it's a monstrous form of flight.

Go on, propose courage, though you're as bloodless
as someone a fever's about to grip: white-knuckled,

chilled by a shadow's flit. You shudder now.
Shame is all that can compel you to pursue

whatever heroics you choose to invoke
—blind faith, a quest, a leap in the dark.

Place your trust in the worst you can imagine,
something vast, freakish, above all beyond.

getting off the ground. Clamber on,
grasp those hulking shoulders. The lion's mane

frames an honest face but the hide is botched,
dragon scales and leopard spots, the tail is forked.

Now you may want holding. Try to cry out.
You'll find your voice is locked in your throat.

God knows what keeps you steady, gets the thing afloat
but it inches away, like a ship backing out of port

till free of the land, then flails its tail like an eel
and you convince yourself that this will propel

you through the atmosphere, that those heavy paws
will paddle the sky like oars. Not sure?

A crack of doubt and your fear will be as pure
as that of all on intimate terms with the air.

Think of Phaethon, his dropped reins, the seared
    heavens
as we still see now; Icarus, as the wax began to soften

and melt, the feathers moult as his father implored
him to fly then heard himself cry, 'You fall...'

Space. Absolute, shapeless, nothing but the long view
and whatever fraudulence it is that carries you.

The beast glides on so slowly, circles with such ease
that you only know you move by the breeze against your
    face

until, from below, the air is disturbed by a whirl of noise,
a torrential roar that starts to twist and hiss and rise

as you cling to the monstrosity you once despised
and beg it to remain in flight. Hold tight.

Screams and flames climb from all sides of a dreadful
    pit,
and you are spiralling down into it.

As when tired of the air, a falcon sinks without bait or
    lure,
his master sighing, 'He will seek no more,'

while the bird wheels indifferently down to land
at some proud distance from his master's hand,

so the beast drops at the foot of a rock and, free of its
    load,
shoots off like an arrow from a bow.

HIGH SUMMER WEIR

Still the day is its own machine and still
you will not speak of it, raise or let fall.

'All life's grandeur' is light on water. So.

Admit now what does not pass and move on
while we are all still here, under the sun.

ERGOT

Not to pin anything down,
it was after all strange country,
but I dreamt a dark river through me
and have become someone else's skin.

Freak convergence, same old story
but on that night in that walled city,
the air was so full of itself
that I grew into him.

Outside the walls, another story
of spurred grain, malfeasant bloom.
A burst husk in a field of rye,
thin-skinned, waterlogged, unready,

bled farouche, corrumpu.
For we must eat bad bread and dance
into the mountain where our souls
will perish or swoon.

AGAINST RHETORIC:
A LETTER TO LORD CHANDOS, 1603

Multum incola fuit anima mea.

    —SIR FRANCIS BACON

That your soul is sometimes strange to you,
is as it is and will become more so.
You are still unbearably young, a prodigy
who weeps like a man of forty
because a beetle must swim coast to coast
in a pail of water, forever. You weep
with the incoherent love of Crassus
for his red-eyed lamprey. 'For me,
everything disintegrated into parts,
those parts again into parts...'
Red-eyed, you despise Crassus.
Your world has fallen out of argument,
a rupture which Sir Francis deploys
as 'broken knowledge', a pause
that finds its echo at the ends of the earth
and is answered by silence in your soul.
There are things multifareous, so much
simultaneous, shapeless, beyond scale...
You are right to give up your *Apophthegmata*.
Caesar wore out his grasp on such gestures.
See his portrait by De Gheyn, an indifferent
history painter, whose virtuoso emperor
dictates three letters while writing a fourth

on horseback. Forget Caesar.
De Gheyn has made a book of small beasts
brought to strangeness, as if glimpsed
before the idea of them has equipped the eye:
a mouse as a powerful whirl of dust,
a frog's back like a sandbank rising in water
swimming with oil; a blue flower cursed
with the preternatural colour of things first.
Steady, Chandos. We are out of rhyme.
Note the flaw in the empty eye.
When things lift away from themselves,
we can do no more in words than meet them
with a similar. Why not remain speechless?
Theaetetus complained to Socrates
of dizziness when asked to see beyond what is
as it is named. His sickness was wonder.

HUSH...

Where the fire of the making of a world
burns itself out, ash banks and rises.

Trees lay down their green.
Roofs lay down their houses.

A boy with a reed for a backbone
shakes in his bed.

It is to him that the mountain has spoken.
He must write in ash what the mountain said.

MINSK

Your great-aunt lost till sprung
by the London Underground inspector's question:

'Where from?' As if bright lines
had led her brothers onto opposite sides

to meet once, thirty years on,
in an airport transit lounge in Miami.

A boom-time armchair prospector
and First Violin of the Cuban Symphony,

reborn under the fixed signs
of Castro and Kennedy,

they fought like lovers, each believing himself
the one left behind in a place he could never

return to, beyond the forest wall
where beekeepers grind stone to brick

in settlement, change into exchange,
where history runs to meet itself

as here, where the headwaters of two rivers
are met by the confluence of two rivers.

A home upon a golden hill
with city-gates of straw and strawheaded children.

THE LAST POSTCARD
after Malevich

I want to give you something as complete
as this house without doors or windows.
It swarms in its rectangle
as busy and inward as an ant hill.
It simmers beneath three chimneys
that are themselves just puffs of smoke,
signals, perhaps,
of frail but conclusive activity.

The red house stands on a green line
that could be grass or a thickening pool.
It widens a little to the left
as if growing or going somewhere.
As for the yellow fence or field
we could climb or walk it,
or take the road that passes through
in a sweep of black, oblivious.

This summer, the years are lining up
like the edge of the world.
All the weight is behind us,
behind the house.
Think of this as the long view:
a resettlement of colour into light
without doors or windows
like this house, where I wish you.

BRIGHT EARTH

arsenic

the apothecary Cranach's gloss
on Adam and Eve:
the cure for a dose

bitumen

a tinge of old master
rising damp, pea-souper

Crystal Palace

nouveau Pompeii
sulphur, cinnabar, lapis lazuli
wall to wall, a wash-out

dung

the glints
lead, shit and a whiff of vinegar
giving a face its sweet and sour

earth

a touch of the worm
under the skin

fiddle

lay that violin on the grass
and tell me again
that a good picture should be brown!

Guimet/Gmelin

a slip of the tongue
and the German lost out
on the prize for synthetic ultramarine
to a native son

heaven

or

ivory

darkening the darks
the flats and sharps

jaspé

the cornerstone
the dappled thing

kermes

crimson sleeps
in the beetle,
is teased from the worm

Lascaux

aurochs, swimming stags
mud in your eye

minium

lead roasted to blistering *naranj,*
for silverfish
a dangerous edge

Napoleon

the bloom
of emerald wallpaper
a last clammy gasp

oil

to paint *en plein air*
a field of linseed,
a poppy, a walnut tree

parsley

with rue and celandine
a salad to cool the flesh,
good for the digestion, the breath

quinine

to set out to conquer malaria
to come home with mauve!

Rhodopos m60a

Yves keeping his powder dry
the blue in his blue

sulphur

mercurial
brimstone
the black stuff

titanium

as radiant as the gods
who could take more heat
than most

urine

the piss of a cow
fed only on mangoes
mopped up, shipped out

Vauquelin

who took the chrome
out of crocoite
the New York taxi-cab
out of Siberian lead

wave

a question of degree
between fourteen and thirty millionths
of an inch

xenon

striplight
pure flare

yolk

Cennini favoured
the undetectable
pallor of town hens

Zaire

a streak of cobalt
and the miner's canary
sang its heart all the way out

'WHAT MAKES FOR THE FULLNESS AND PERFECTION OF LIFE'

It only came back when I stopped to consider
the small ways in which a garden holds water,
and paused halfway through the door in suspense
like the dream which, early that morning,
had flicked its magnificent tail then was gone.

III

A DRINK OF GLASS

Petersburg breathed through Finland...
One travelled there to think out
what one could not think out in Petersburg.

—OSIP MANDELSTAM

Kaamos

This is the time to live quietly,
to build nothing and tell stories...

Here, the bedrock is older than life
on earth. It carries no trace of death,
no methane or anthracite, nothing to burn.
Firey capillaries of copper, cobalt, gold
—how to keep warm?
My cold heart arrests its blood
like the sun taking its colour down.
I breathe ice.
They say my lungs might bloom.

I never quite wake but go slowly
and my thoughts are as careful
and stiff as the tick of my pulse.
I feel patient, honest and kindly
and cannot crack a smile.

Arctic winter has set in my body
like a drink of glass. Blown,
I take place outside myself

where it's almost always almost dark
and black clusters at the northern horizon
like iron filings drawn to the Great Nail
strangers dream they find.

It's the tip of the axis
where the wind blows only to and from
the south, and wherever you go is south,
and nothing will rise or set
and time unspools like a frozen river
—a blank tape measure
on which to write any number of numbers.

I meet long looks in straight faces.
Forest is their biggest secret.
It grows in their hearts.

Steam

I climb out of layers, wash off layers, take out my eyes.
Three times, back and forth in growing separation.
Under cold water, skin and bones; in the heat, all heart.
The coals mutter like gods locked in the earth.
When I douse them, they blurt. They want to tell,
they want to tell and I breathe them...

It's not enough, only a few small steps
like those of the women picking their way
along a glazed jetty through sectioned light.
They fold their robes, test each rung,
half-enter a pool punched in three feet of ice.
Each swims a neat circle, wearing slippers and gloves.

Blue Field

A flood as the day releases
and the whole snow world
is neither wet nor deep, but primary.
Colour so inherent, it does not fall
but rises from my skin,
the snow, the trees, the road.
This blue isn't built or grown.
It has no tissue, nothing
to touch or taste or bring to mind
a memory, no iris or artery,
no gentian, aconite or anemone,
no slate, plum, oil-spill or gun,
no titanium or turquoise,
no mercury or magnesium,
no phosphorus, sapphire or silver foil,
no duck egg or milk jug,
no chambray, denim or navy,
no indigo, octopus ink, no ink,
no element. The blue moment,
'sininen hetki' in a language that claims
no relation but greets in passing
picture blue, cyan. Ultraviolet
twilight, higher than the heaven
of swimming or flying—no splash.
A time without clouded objects,

in which you might become the glass
you swallowed through cold.
Light draws back
behind the rim of the eye as it closes.
I keep my distance, as things turn blue
through stillness and distance,
as everything blue is distant.

Sisu

To persevere in hope of summer.
To adapt to its broken promise.
To love winter.

To sleep.

To love winter.
To adapt to its broken promise.
To persevere in hope of summer.

THE LAND OF GIVING IN
Midsummer, Lofoten Islands

Edda

Winter light is in frozen water,
a flood that whites out road and river
and though you can't see over or under,
it locks in place.

Now it is summer.
Thin-skinned islands hover.
There are no islands in winter
and nothing as dark as this deep water.

Ibsen

Pale hours in a town on the edge
where tractor-tyres bolster the dock
and the airport, fishery and church
arrived flat-packed on the back of a truck.

I can't see the sun that never sets,
only a low tin sky tamped down
like a caravan roof. It lets in rain
as if the people of the town,

doubled over by high summer,
had passed a vote to punch out the light
and laid down bets on who would get
first glimpse of night.

Vaerøy

The man filming a map of the islands does not look up
as we sail among them. Hundreds.
All the small bones of feet and hands.
What god is this we travel for hours,
getting no further than the tips of his fingers?
Why land on this broken knuckle
where a mountain divides the sun?
Night, day, I edge up and down the track,
walk, look, sit and look
at the furthest islands extending the plane.
Their cliffs shear off light, set them afloat.
My eyes hurt to have to see the earth curve so.

Silica

This beach is a ledge of pulverised light,
the ashes of someone barely there
in the first place: a wraith,

hatched from stones pounded over and over,
who made herself in the image of shells,
emptied and tempered, translucent hulls

and made herself in the image of bones,
dislocated, blanched and cold
like the trail of femur, socket and jaw

washed up on this far shore.
A child's head on a snapped neck,
more clear than human.

Bird Walk

White nights feather my mind.
I am a giant of sleeplessness, as high
as the cliff where auks lay teetering eggs
which droop roughly, like tears.

They won't roll. My mind rolls.
To sleep, I must think like the birds
in camouflage, decoys and patrols.

Redshanks storm the grass, post sentries
on telegraph poles, as highly strung
as the oystercatchers all in a flap,
outcrying their young to mislead crows
who shrug and brag and lunge.

At three a.m., a black cormorant dives.
A needle, a nightfall, it closes my eyes.

Heliotropical

Brightness burns midsummer's eve
fires to air: they crackle, invisible.

At midnight, the sun glides into reverse
like Anna backwards, a god having second thoughts.

It looks easy, but hurts.
I'm strung out on a fifty-foot shadow,

up to my knees in dandelion clocks
which glow like liquid worlds of sleep.

A dip below the surface of sleep
and then hours of ecstatic frenetic.

Light pumps into the room, pumps into me,
leaving nothing to fill.

My heart bursts with joy, every cell,
and the light comes still.

The Boat Back into the Dark

We stop to pick up a hunting party:
angels with horns, beards and guns,
trophies lashed to their handlebars.

We skirt the maelström.
The sea leans and slops and changes.
The angels nibble spiral ices.

The captain turns the radio on.
'The Green, Green Grass of Home'.
I try not to sing along.

ACKNOWLEDGMENTS

Acknowledgments are due to the editors of the following: *Europe, Frankfurter Allgemeine Zeitung, Grand Street, The Guardian, Heat, Last Words, Literary Imagination, London Review of Books, Metre, The New Yorker, New Writing 8* and *9* (British Council), *Po&sie, Poetry Review, The Red Wheelbarrow, Schreibheft, Thumbscrew* and *The Times Literary Supplement.*

Several of the poems were broadcast on BBC Radio 3 and 4. 'The Flight of Geryon' was commissioned for Poetry International 2000, 'Foxtrot' was written for The Poetry Proms 2001, 'Bright Earth' for The Royal Institution/Gulbenkian Foundation. 'Against Rhetoric' was commissioned for *'Lieber Lord Chandos': Antworten auf einen Brief,* Roland Spahr, Hubert Spiegel and Oliver Vogel (eds.), published by S. Fischer, 2002.

The lines from Rilke on page 29 are from the second of the *Duino Elegies* and were translated by J. B. Leishman and Stephen Spender.

The author is grateful to the National Endowment for Science, Technology and the Arts (NESTA) for a fellowship.

With particular thanks to Tim Dee for the bird walks.

9/09/05   **DATE DUE** L L J

WITHDRAWN

GAYLORD   PRINTED IN U.S.A